GUIDELINES FOR THE Celebration of the Sacraments with Persons with Disabilities

Revised Edition

Our Sunday Visitor
Huntington, Indiana

The document *Guidelines for the Celebration of the Sacraments with Persons with Disabilities (Revised Edition)* was developed by the Committee on Divine Worship of the United States Conference of Catholic Bishops (USCCB). It was approved by the full body of the USCCB at its June 2017 General Meeting. It has been directed for publication by the undersigned.

Msgr. J. Brian Bransfield
General Secretary, USCCB

ISBN: 978-1-63966-296-8 (Inventory No. T2953)
eISBN: 978-1-63966-297-5

First printing, September 2017
Current printing, 2024, published by OSV, Our Sunday Visitor, 200 Noll Plaza, Huntington, IN 46750; 1-800-348-3440; www.osv.com

Cover photo: Adobestock

Printed in the United States of America

The Church continues to affirm the dignity of every human being, and to grow in knowledge and understanding of the gifts and needs of her members who live with disabilities. Likewise, the Church recognizes that every parish community includes members with disabilities, and earnestly desires their active participation. All members of the Body of Christ are uniquely called by God by virtue of their Baptism. In light of this call, the Church seeks to support all in their growth in holiness, and to encourage all in their vocations. Participating in, and being nourished by, the grace of the sacraments is essential to this growth in holiness. Catholic adults and children with disabilities, and their families, earnestly desire full and meaningful participation in the sacramental life of the Church.

In this regard, as it issues a revised and expanded *Guidelines for the Celebration of the Sacraments with Persons with Disabilities*, the United States Conference of Catholic Bishops wishes to reiterate what was said in previous pastoral statements on this issue:

> It is essential that all forms of the liturgy be completely accessible to persons with disabilities, since these forms are the essence of the spiritual tie that binds the Christian community together. To exclude members

of the parish from these celebrations of the life of the Church, even by passive omission, is to deny the reality of that community. Accessibility involves far more than physical alterations to parish buildings. Realistic provision must be made for Catholics with disabilities to participate fully in the Eucharist and other liturgical celebrations.[1]

Preface

Catholics with disabilities, as well as those who minister to or with them, often point out that pastoral practice with regard to the celebration of the sacraments varies greatly from diocese to diocese, even from parish to parish. Inconsistencies arise in such areas as the provision of sign language interpreters and captioning for persons who are deaf, in the accessibility of church facilities for persons with mobility needs, and in the availability of catechetical programs for persons with intellectual, developmental, and other disabilities. Pastoral inconsistencies may occur in other areas as well.

The inconsistencies in pastoral practice often arise from distinct yet overlapping causes. Some result from a misunderstanding

1 *Pastoral Statement of US Catholic Bishops on Persons with Disabilities* (November 1978, revised 1989), 23.

about the nature of disabilities. Others arise from an uncertainty about the appropriate application of church law toward persons with disabilities. Others are born out of fear, misunderstanding, or unfamiliarity. Still others seem to be the result of the real or perceived limitations of a parish's or diocese's available resources.

These guidelines were developed to address many of the concerns raised by persons with disabilities and their families and advocates, and also clergy and other pastoral ministers, for greater consistency in pastoral practice in the celebration of the sacraments throughout the country. With this objective in view, and with the desire to meet the spiritual, sacramental, and pastoral needs of persons with disabilities, the guidelines draw upon the Church's ritual books, its canonical tradition, and its experience in ministering to or with persons with disabilities in order to dispel misunderstandings that may impede sound pastoral practice in the celebration of the sacraments. It is our hope that the guidelines will enhance diocesan policies already in existence.

The bishops of the United States offer the *Guidelines for the Celebration of the Sacraments with Persons with Disabilities* in order to give a more concrete expression to our longstanding concern for "realistic provision" for the means of access to full sacramental participation for Catholic persons with disabilities.[2]

While they do not address every conceivable situation that may arise in pastoral practice, the guidelines present a set of general principles to provide access to the sacraments for persons with disabilities. Diocesan staff, pastoral leaders, catechists, parishioners, health care workers, and all those who minister to or with Catholics with disabilities are invited and encouraged to reflect upon and utilize these guidelines in their continuing effort to bring Christ's healing message and call to justice to the world.

I. GENERAL PRINCIPLES

1. All human beings are equal in dignity in the sight of God. Moreover, by reason of their Baptism, all Catholics also share the same divine calling.

2. Catholics with disabilities have a right to participate in the sacraments as fully as other members of the local ecclesial

2 The *Guidelines* were developed specifically for the Latin Church. They may be of assistance, however, to all Churches *sui iuris* in the United States, following the necessary adaptation to reflect the particular traditions, pastoral life, and requirements of the *Code of Canons of the Eastern Churches*.

community.[3] "Sacred ministers cannot deny the sacraments to those who seek them at appropriate times, are properly disposed, and are not prohibited by law from receiving them."[4]

3. Parish sacramental celebrations should be accessible to persons with disabilities and open to their full, active, and conscious participation, according to their capacity. Pastoral ministers should not presume to know the needs of persons with disabilities, but should rather—before all else—consult with them or their advocates before making determinations about the accessibility of a parish's facilities and the availability of its programs, policies, and ministries. Full accessibility should be the goal for every parish, and these adaptations are to be an ordinary part of the liturgical life of the parish.[5]

4. Since the parish is the center of the Christian experience for most Catholics, pastors and other parish ministers should make every effort to provide for all Catholics with disabilities who reside within a parish's boundaries. Special effort should be made to reach out to and welcome all parishioners, including persons

---

3 See *Codex Iuris Canonici* (CIC), c. 835, §4.

4 CIC, c. 843, §1.

5 See Pope Benedict XVI, Post-Synodal Apostolic Exhortation *Sacramentum caritatis* (February 22, 2007), 58.

with disabilities who live independently, with their families, in institutions, or in other living arrangements. Pastoral visitation, the parish census, and the diverse forms of parish and diocesan social communication are just a few of the many ways in which the pastoral staff can work toward the inclusion of all parishioners in the parish's sacramental life.

5. Pastors are responsible to provide evangelization, catechetical formation, and sacramental preparation for parishioners with disabilities,[6] and dioceses are encouraged to establish appropriate support services to assist pastors in this duty. Persons with disabilities, their advocates and their families, as well as those knowledgeable in serving those with disabilities can make a most valuable contribution to these efforts. Parish catechetical and sacramental preparation programs may need to be adapted for some parishioners with disabilities, though, as much as possible, persons with disabilities should be integrated into the ordinary programs. They should not be segregated for specialized catechesis unless their disabilities make it impossible for them to participate in the basic catechetical program.[7]

---

6 See CIC, c. 777, 4°.

7 See *National Directory for Catechesis* (NDC) (Washington, DC: USCCB, 2005), 49.

Even in those cases, participation in parish life is encouraged in all ways possible.

6. Having received the sacraments, which "contribute in the greatest way to establish, strengthen, and manifest ecclesiastical communion,"[8] persons with disabilities, like all other parishioners, should be encouraged to participate in all levels of pastoral ministry that are available and for which they are qualified. For example, members of the laity are often needed to perform various services or functions in liturgical celebrations, particularly in the celebration of Mass. In choosing those who will be invited to use their gifts in service to the parish community, the parish pastoral staff and lay volunteers, including ushers and liturgical ministers, should be mindful of extending Christ's welcoming invitation to qualified parishioners with disabilities. Like others, Catholics with disabilities are not only recipients of the Gospel, but are also called to proclaim it and to be witnesses to its truth.[9]

7. The creation of a fully accessible parish reaches beyond mere physical accommodation to encompass the attitudes of all parishioners toward persons with disabilities. All members of the faith community

8 CIC, c. 840.

9 See NDC, 49.

have a role to play in the invitation, welcome, and inclusion of people with disabilities. Pastoral ministers are encouraged to foster attitudes and a parish culture, and to develop informational materials, aimed at forming a community of believers known for its joyful inclusion of all of God's people around the table of the Lord.

8. Difficult situations may be encountered by those making pastoral decisions. Dioceses are encouraged to establish appropriate policies for handling such instances, which respect the rights of all involved, and which ensure the necessary provision of evaluation and recourse.

II. PARTICULAR SACRAMENTS

Baptism

9. Through the Sacrament of Baptism the faithful are incorporated into Christ and into his Church. They obtain forgiveness of all their sins and are formed into God's people. They become a new creation and are called, rightly, the children of God.[10]

10 See *Christian Initiation*, General Introduction, 1-2; see CIC, c. 849.

10. So that Baptism may be seen as a sacrament of the Church's faith and of admittance into the People of God, it should be celebrated ordinarily in the parish church on a Sunday or, if possible, at the Easter Vigil.[11] The Church, made present in the local community, has an important role to play in the Baptism of all of its members. Before and after the celebration of the sacrament, the baptized have the right to the love and help of the community.[12]

11. Because it is the sacrament of universal salvation, Baptism is to be made available to all who freely ask for it, are properly disposed, and are not prohibited by law from receiving it. In the case of infants and those who cannot request it for themselves, Baptism may be deferred only when there is no reason for hoping that the person will be brought up in the Catholic faith.[13] Disability, of itself, is never a reason for deferring Baptism. Persons who lack the use of reason are to be baptized provided at least one parent or guardian consents to it.[14]

Parents who receive a prenatal diagnosis of a life-threatening condition should receive the support they need to assure that their child will be baptized "without

---

11 See CIC, cc. 856 and 857.

12 See *Rite of Baptism for Children*, 4 and 10.

13 See CIC, c. 868, §1, 2°.

14 See CIC, cc. 868, §1, 1° and 852.

delay."[15] Indeed, priests, deacons, and other pastoral ministers should provide spiritual and emotional support to families who have received any difficult prenatal diagnosis and offer on-going support before and after the birth of a child, with special concern in the event of the death of a child.

12. Either personally or through others, the pastor is to see to it that the parents of an infant with a disability, those who take the place of the parents, and those who will fulfill the function of godparent are properly instructed as to the meaning of the Sacrament of Baptism and the obligations attached to it. If possible, either the pastor or a member of the parish community should visit with the family, offering them the strength and support of the community, which rejoices at the gift of new life, and which promises to nurture the faith of its new member. It is recommended that preparation programs for Baptism gather several families together so that they may commonly be formed by pastoral direction and prayer, and so that they may be strengthened by mutual support.[16]

13. "The Initiation of catechumens is a gradual process that takes place within the

15 CIC, c. 867, §2.

16 See CIC, c. 851, 2°.

community of the faithful."[17] Adults and children of catechetical age with disabilities should be welcomed into all stages and rites of the initiation process. If the catechumen is of catechetical age, the rites may be adapted according to need.[18] In these cases, catechesis for persons with disabilities must be adapted in content and method to their particular situations.[19] Like others, adults and children of catechetical age with disabilities should normally receive the Sacraments of Baptism, Confirmation, and Eucharist in a single celebration.[20]

14. A sponsor is to be chosen who will assist the catechumen in preparing for the Sacraments of Initiation and, as such, will have a special role in fostering the faith life of the catechumen. Likewise, godparents are to be chosen who will guide the catechumen through the final preparation for Baptism, and to assist the newly-baptized adult or child through the rest of their Christian life. The same person may be both sponsor and godparent. Catholics with disabilities may serve as sponsors and godparents, and like others who fulfill these

17 RCIA, Introduction, 4.

18 See CIC, cc. 851, 1° and 852, §1; see RCIA, 34 and 35.

19 See NDC, 49.

20 See *National Statutes for the Catechumenate* (NSC) (Washington, DC: NCCB, 1986), 14.

roles, they are to be carefully chosen and formed for these responsibilities.[21]

Confirmation

15. "Those who have been baptized continue on the path of Christian Initiation through the Sacrament of Confirmation." In this way, they receive the Holy Spirit, conforming them more perfectly to Christ and strengthening them so that they may "bear witness to Christ for the building up of his Body in faith and charity."[22]

16. Parents, those who care for persons with disabilities, and shepherds of souls—especially pastors—are to see to it that the faithful who have been baptized receive the formation needed for the Sacrament of Confirmation and approach it at the appropriate time.[23] "The diocesan bishop is obliged to take care that the Sacrament of Confirmation is conferred on subjects who properly and reasonably seek it."[24]

17. Confirmation is to be conferred on the faithful between the age of discretion (which is about the age of seven) and about sixteen years of age, within the limits determined by the diocesan bishop,

---

21 See CIC, c. 872 and 874.

22 *Order of Confirmation*, 1-2; see CIC, c. 879.

23 See CIC, c. 890.

24 CIC, c. 885, §1.

or when there is a danger of death, or in the judgment of the minister a grave cause urges otherwise.[25]

18. All baptized Catholics who possess the use of reason may receive the Sacrament of Confirmation if they are "suitably instructed, properly disposed and able to renew the baptismal promises."[26] Persons who because of intellectual or developmental disabilities may never attain the use of reason can receive the Sacrament of Confirmation and should be encouraged either directly or, if necessary, through their parents, to receive it. It is important that they receive the pastoral guidance needed, along with the welcome and embrace of the whole community of faith. To the degree possible, those with disabilities should be included along with others during the preparation and celebration of the sacrament. At times, pastoral need may necessitate an accommodated setting and a simpler manner.

19. A sponsor for the one to be confirmed should be present. The sponsor assists the confirmed person on the continuing path

---

25 See United States Conference of Catholic Bishops (USCCB), Decree implementing canon 891 (August 21, 2001): *http://www.usccb.org/beliefs-and-teachings/what-we-believe/canon-law/complementary-norms/canon-891-age-for-confirmation.cfm.*

26 CIC, c. 889.

of Christian Initiation.[27] For this reason, it is desirable that one of the godparents chosen for Baptism be the sponsor for Confirmation.[28]

20. When those with disabilities who are already baptized Christians desire to become Catholic, they should participate in the *Rite of Reception of Baptized Christians into the Full Communion of the Catholic Church*, which normally includes the reception of the Sacraments of Confirmation and Eucharist.[29]

Eucharist

21. The Eucharist is the most august sacrament, in which Christ the Lord himself is contained, offered, and received, and by which the Church constantly lives and grows. It is the summit and the source of all Christian worship and life, signifying and effecting the unity of the People of God, providing spiritual nourishment for the recipient, and achieving the building up of the Body of Christ.[30] The celebration of the Eucharist is the center of the entire Christian life.

---

27 See CIC, c. 892.

28 See CIC, c. 893, §2.

29 See RCIA, 473-498; see NSC, 35.

30 See CIC, c. 897.

22. Parents or guardians, together with pastors, are to see to it that children who have reached the use of reason are correctly prepared and are nourished by the Eucharist as early as possible. Pastors are to be vigilant lest any children come to the Holy Banquet who have not reached the use of reason or whom they judge are not sufficiently disposed.[31] It is important to note, however, that the criterion for reception of Holy Communion is the same for persons with intellectual and developmental disabilities as for all persons, namely, that the person be able to "distinguish the body of Christ from ordinary food," even if this recognition is evidenced through manner, gesture, or reverential silence rather than verbally.[32] Pastors are encouraged to consult with parents, those who take the place of parents, diocesan personnel involved with disability issues, psychologists, religious educators, and other experts in making their judgment. If it is determined that a parishioner who is disabled is not ready to receive the sacrament, great care is to be taken in explaining the reasons for this decision. Cases of doubt should be resolved in favor of the right of the Catholic to receive the sacrament. The

31 See CIC, c. 914.

32 CIC, c. 913, §2; see Pope Benedict XVI, Post-Synodal Apostolic Exhortation *Sacramentum caritatis* (February 22, 2007), 58.

existence of a disability is not considered in and of itself as disqualifying a person from receiving Holy Communion.

23. Given the paramount significance of the Eucharist in the lives of the faithful, and in light of medical and technological advancements that affect Catholics with disabilities, new questions have arisen regarding the reception of Holy Communion, and circumstances that were once rare have even become relatively common. Clergy and extraordinary ministers of Holy Communion are encouraged to become familiar with the needs of their parishioners. In many instances, simple accommodations can be very helpful, and should be embraced by all at the parish level.

24. Catholics who require nourishment through feeding tubes are encouraged to receive Holy Communion, as are all the Catholic faithful. Christ is sacramentally present under each of the species, and Holy Communion can be received under the species of bread or wine alone.[33] Since the full presence of Christ and his sanctifying grace are found in even the smallest piece of the consecrated host or in a mere drop of the consecrated wine, the norm of receiving through the mouth remains the

33 See *Catechism of the Catholic Church*, 1390; CIC, c. 925.

same for those who otherwise use a feeding tube for sustenance, and Holy Communion is not to be administered through a feeding tube. For these communicants it will commonly be possible to place one or a few drops of the Precious Blood on the tongue. Clergy and pastoral ministers are encouraged to use these guidelines and consult with physicians, family members, and other experts on a case-by-case basis, to determine how those who use feeding tubes may avail themselves of the abundant fruits of Holy Communion. Specialized instruction for extraordinary ministers of Holy Communion is to be provided as required.

25. Catholics with Celiac Sprue Disease or other conditions that make them gluten intolerant should be given the opportunity to receive a small fragment of a regular host, and made aware of the options to receive a low-gluten host or to receive under the form of wine alone. In the event of intolerance to gluten and wine, mustum may also be an option, with the approval of the local ordinary.[34] Clergy and extraordinary ministers of Holy Communion need to be aware of the possibility of cross-contamination and related issues in order to plan for

---

34 See Congregation for the Doctrine of the Faith, *Circular Letter to all Presidents of the Episcopal Conferences concerning the use of low-gluten altar breads and mustum as matter for the celebration of the Eucharist* (July 24, 2003), C-1.

the safe administration of the sacred species to Catholics with gluten intolerance. For example, the chalice given to a person with gluten intolerance should not contain a particle of the host, and low-gluten altar breads should never be intermingled with regular altar breads. As people may feel self-conscious at the prospect of needing special arrangements for the reception of Holy Communion, pastoral sensitivity in this area is particularly important.

26. When baptized Catholics who have been regular communicants develop advanced Alzheimer's or other age-related dementias, there is to be a presumption in favor of the individual's ability to distinguish between Holy Communion and regular food. Holy Communion should continue to be offered as long as possible, and ministers are called to carry out their ministry with a special patience. If swallowing becomes particularly difficult, decisions regarding the continued reception of Holy Communion may have to be faced. This pastoral decision is to be made on a case-by-case basis, in consultation with the individual, those closest to him or her, physicians, and the pastor.

Reconciliation

27. In the Sacrament of Penance, the Catholic faithful obtain from the mercy of God pardon for their sins. At the same time, they are reconciled with the Church, which they have wounded by their sins and which works for their conversion by charity, example, and prayer.[35]

28. Only those who have the use of reason are capable of committing mortal sin. Nevertheless, even young children and persons with intellectual disabilities often are conscious of committing acts that are sinful to some degree and may experience a sense of guilt and sorrow. As long as the individual is capable of having a sense of contrition for having committed sin, even if he or she cannot describe the sin precisely in words, the person may receive sacramental absolution. Those with profound intellectual disabilities, who cannot experience even minimal contrition, may be invited to participate in penitential services with the rest of the community to the extent of their ability.

29. In the case of individuals who are nonverbal or have minimal verbal communication ability, sorrow for sin is to be accepted

35 See Second Vatican Council, Dogmatic Constitution on the Church *Lumen Gentium*, 11; see CIC, c. 959.

even if this repentance is expressed through some gesture rather than verbally. Many Catholics experience significant communication difficulties related to autism spectrum disorder, traumatic brain injury, post-stroke complications, and other conditions. Catholics with significant communication disorders may be permitted to make their confessions using the communication system with which they are most fluent. Individuals preparing for the sacrament are to be taught to be as independent as possible in the use of their communication system to allow for the norm of private reception of the sacrament.

Confessors are encouraged to work with families and individuals to familiarize themselves with various alternative communication options to ensure that all who desire to celebrate this sacrament may do so, provided that the seal of confession is properly safeguarded. In posing questions and in the assignment of penances the confessor is to proceed with prudence and discretion, mindful that he is at once judge and healer, minister of divine justice within the context of divine mercy.[36]

30. Catholics who are deaf should have the opportunity to confess to a priest able to communicate with them in sign language,

---

36 See CIC, cc. 978, §1, 979, and 981.

if sign language is their primary means of communication. They may also confess through an approved sign language interpreter of their choice.[37] The interpreter has the obligation to observe secrecy.[38] When neither a priest with signing skills nor a sign language interpreter is available, Catholics who are deaf should be permitted to make their confession in writing or through the use of an appropriate portable electronic communication device that can be passed back and forth between the penitent and confessor. The written or digital materials are to be returned to the penitent and properly destroyed or deleted.

31. Pastoral consideration needs to be given to those for whom reception of the sacrament within the confines of the confessional may be problematic. While this would certainly constitute a just cause for Reconciliation outside of a confessional, every effort should be made to ensure that penitents who are wheelchair users have access to both face-to-face and private confessionals, with due regard for the right of the priest to insist on confession behind a fixed screen.[39]

---

37 See CIC, c. 990.

38 See CIC, cc. 983, §2 and 1388, §2.

39 See CIC, c. 964; see USCCB, Decree implementing canon 964, §2 (October 20, 2000): *http://www.usccb.org/beliefs-and-teachings/what-we-believe/canon-law/complementary-norms/canon-964-2-the-confessional.cfm*; see Pontifical Council for

Anointing of the Sick

32. Through the Anointing of the Sick, the Church commends to the suffering and glorified Lord the faithful who are seriously ill, so that they may be relieved of their suffering and be saved.[40]

33. Those who have the care of souls and those who are close to the sick are to see to it that the faithful who are in danger due to sickness or old age are supported by the Sacrament of the Anointing of the Sick at the appropriate time.[41]

34. Since disability does not necessarily indicate an illness, Catholics with disabilities should receive the Anointing of the Sick on the same basis and under the same circumstances as any other member of the Christian faithful.[42]

35. The Anointing of the Sick may be conferred if the recipient has sufficient use of reason to be strengthened by the sacrament, or if the sick person has lost the use of reason and would have asked for the sacrament while in control of his or her faculties.[43] If there is doubt as to whether the

---

the Interpretation of Legislative Texts, Response, July 7, 1998: *Acta Apostolicæ Sedis* 90 (1998), 711.

40 See CIC, c. 998.

41 See CIC, c. 1001.

42 See CIC, c. 1004.

43 See *Pastoral Care of the Sick: Rites of Anointing and Viaticum,*

sick person has attained the use of reason, the sacrament is to be conferred.[44] Persons with disabilities may at times be served best through inclusion in communal celebrations of the Anointing of the Sick.[45]

Holy Orders

36. By divine institution, some among the Christian faithful are constituted sacred ministers through the Sacrament of Orders. They are consecrated and deputed to shepherd the People of God, each in accord with his own grade of orders.[46]

37. The existence of a physical disability is not considered in and of itself as disqualifying a person from Holy Orders. However, candidates for ordination must possess the necessary spiritual, physical, human, moral, intellectual, emotional, and psychological qualities and abilities to fulfill the ministerial functions of the order they receive.[47] The proper bishop or competent major superior makes the judgment that candidates are suited for ordained ministry in the Church.[48] Cases are to be decided on an individual basis and in light of pasto-

---

12 and 14.

44 See CIC, c. 1005.

45 See CIC, c. 1002.

46 See CIC, c. 1008.

47 See CIC, cc. 1029 and 1041, 1°.

48 See CIC, cc. 241, §1; 1025, §2; 1029; and 1051, 1°.

ral judgment and the opinions of diocesan personnel and other experts involved with disability issues.

38. Diocesan vocations offices and offices for ministry with persons with disabilities should provide counseling, informational resources, and reasonable accommodations for men with disabilities who are discerning a vocation to serve the Church through one of the ordained ministries.

39. In preparation for responsible leadership in ordained ministry, the diocesan bishop or major superior is to see to it that the formation of all students in the seminary includes awareness of and experience with persons with disabilities. Formation personnel should consult with persons with disabilities, parents, psychologists, religious educators, and other experts in the adaptation of programs for ministerial formation related to disabilities. Indeed, these *Guidelines* might even be part of the course of studies in seminaries and in ongoing formation of the clergy.

40. Some men with disabilities already serve the Church as bishops, priests, or deacons. Clergy who have or acquire a disability are to have access to resources and accommodations that will aid them in continuing in their ministry.

Marriage

41. In the Sacrament of Matrimony, Christians signify and participate in the mystery of the unity and fruitful love which exists between Christ and his Church. They help each other to attain holiness in their married life and in the rearing and education of their children.[49]

42. "All persons who are not prohibited by law can contract marriage."[50]

43. Pastors of souls should make the necessary provisions to ensure the inclusion of persons with disabilities in marriage preparation programs. Through this preparation all couples may become predisposed toward holiness and to the duties of their new state. In developing diocesan policies, the local ordinary should consult with men and women of proven experience and skill in understanding the emotional, physical, spiritual, and psychological needs of persons with intellectual disabilities.[51] Including persons with disabilities in sponsor couple programs is an especially effective way of supporting both the needs and the gifts of couples preparing for marriage.

---

49 See *Order of Celebrating Matrimony*, 8.

50 CIC, c. 1058.

51 See CIC, cc. 1063, 2° and 1064.

44. Couples with intellectual or developmental disabilities who believe they are called to the vocation of married life are encouraged to seek counsel by discussing the Sacrament of Matrimony with their families and pastors. For matrimonial consent to be valid, it is necessary that the contracting parties possess a sufficient use of reason; that they be free of any grave lack of discretion affecting their judgment about the rights and duties to which they are committing themselves; and that they have the mental capacity to assume the essential obligations of the married state.[52] It is also necessary that the parties understand that marriage is a permanent union and is ordered to the good of the spouses and the procreation and education of children.[53] Pastors and other clergy are to decide cases on an individual basis and in light of pastoral judgment based upon consultation with diocesan personnel involved with disability issues, and canonical, medical, and other experts.

A physical disability, in and of itself, does not necessarily constitute an impediment to marriage. Medical and canonical opinions should be sought in determining the presence of any impediments to marriage. It should be noted, moreover, that

52 See CIC, c. 1095.
53 See CIC, cc. 1096 and 1055, §1.

paraplegia does not always imply impotence, nor the permanence of such a condition, and it is not in itself an impediment. In case of doubt with regard to impotence, marriage may not be impeded.[54]

45. Catholics who are deaf are to be offered the opportunity to express their matrimonial consent in sign language, if sign language is their primary means of communication.[55] Marriage may also be contracted with the assistance of a sign language interpreter whose trustworthiness has been certified by the pastor.[56] Likewise, those who are nonverbal or have minimal verbal communication ability should be offered the opportunity to express their matrimonial consent using the communication system with which they are most fluent.

46. Pastoral care for married persons extends throughout their lives. By their care and example, the entire ecclesial community bears witness to the fact that the matrimonial state may be maintained in a Christian spirit and make progress toward perfection. Special care is to be taken to include parishioners with disabilities in parish programs aimed at assisting

54 See CIC, c. 1084, §2.
55 See CIC, c. 1104, §2.
56 See CIC, c. 1106.

and nourishing married couples in leading holier and fuller lives within their families.[57]

As people live longer, more will experience loss of mental and physical capabilities, including Alzheimer's and other age-related dementias. The faith community must minister both to the spouse whose body or mind begins to fail and also to the spouse who becomes the caregiver. The witness to their matrimonial commitment "in good times and in bad, in sickness and in health"[58] should be recognized and honored by the whole faith community. Adult children who care for their parents also deserve the community's support and encouragement.

57 See CIC, c. 1063, 4°.

58 *Order of Celebrating Matrimony*, 62.

Conclusion

These guidelines are presented to all who are involved in liturgical, pastoral, and catechetical ministry. All persons with disabilities have gifts to contribute to the whole Church. When persons with disabilities are embraced and welcomed, and invited to participate fully in all aspects of parish community life, the Body of Christ is more complete. "The Church owes persons with disabilities her best efforts in order to ensure that they are able to hear the Gospel of Christ, receive the sacraments, and grow in their faith in the fullest and richest manner possible."[59]

---

59 NDC, 49.

